RESURRECTION

Living as People of the Risen Lord

10 STUDIES FOR INDIVIDUALS OR GROUPS

LifeGuide®
BIBLE STUDIES

KRISTIE BERGLUND

IVP Connect
An imprint of InterVarsity Press
Downers Grove, Illinois

InterVarsity Press
P.O. Box 1400, Downers Grove, IL 60515-1426
ivpress.com
email@ivpress.com

InterVarsity Press® is the book-publishing division of InterVarsity Christian Fellowship/USA®, a
movement of students and faculty active on campus at hundreds of universities, colleges and schools
of nursing in the United States of America, and a member movement of the International Fellowship
of Evangelical Students. For information about local and regional activities, visit intervarsity.org.

LifeGuide® is a registered trademark of InterVarsity Christian Fellowship.

All Scripture quotations, unless otherwise indicated, are taken from THE HOLY BIBLE, NEW
INTERNATIONAL VERSION®, NIV® Copyright © 1973, 1978, 1984, 2011 by Biblica, Inc.™ Used
by permission. All rights reserved worldwide.

While all stories in this book are true, some names and identifying information in this book have
been changed to protect the privacy of the individuals involved.

Cover image: © Nilufer Barin / Trevillion Images

ISBN 978-0-8308-3105-0

Printed in the United States of America ♾

green
press
INITIATIVE
As a member of the Green Press Initiative, InterVarsity Press is committed to
protecting the environment and to the responsible use of natural resources. To learn
more, visit greenpressinitiative.org.

P	15	14	13	12	11	10	9	8
Y	28	27	26	25	24	23	22	

Contents

Getting the Most Out of *Resurrection*

The resurrection of Jesus Christ changed everything. When dawn broke on that first Easter morning, the sun rose on an entirely new world. The very fabric of creation had been transformed. The direction of history had been altered. The power of death had been broken. Life was victorious.

How are we to live in the light of that glorious day? How does Christ's great victory play out in our everyday lives? As people of the risen Lord, our identity and calling are rooted in the resurrection. We are the people of God's new creation living in the midst of a world still reeling from the longstanding effects of sin and death. As we receive healing and experience our own transformation in Christ, we show forth his risen life to others. Our renewed lives proclaim his resurrection, and those around us are drawn to the everliving source of that warmth and light.

These ten studies will explore the significance of Christ's resurrection for our everyday lives. We will see how the prophet Ezekiel spoke of a day of restoration and new beginning for God's people when they had all but given up hope. We will boldly approach Christ along with Jairus and the bleeding woman, trusting that he alone has the life-giving power to heal the sick and raise the dead. We will weep with Mary and Martha outside the tomb of Lazarus, and marvel at the way Christ's love reaches beyond the grave. We will walk with the two disciples on the road to Emmaus and discover that Christ has been with us the whole time. We will run with the women from the tomb to tell the disciples the great news and learn to take our place in the great mission of Christ to the world. We will hear Peter's bold testimony to the resurrection and join him in steadfast allegiance to the true Lord and King of all. With the Corinthian church we will discover that our life and work in the present age hold great meaning for our risen life to come. With the church at Rome we will learn that the Spirit of the risen Lord frees us from our bondage to sin and death. Along with the Colossians we will discover that the Christian life is lived through participation in Christ's resurrection and shows forth in the new clothing we wear. Finally, with John we will watch as God makes all things new and finally banishes death from his world.

My hope is that as we reflect together on the wonder of our lives as the people of the risen Lord, we will more deeply embrace God's promises to us and more fully embody his resurrected life for all the world to see.

Suggestions for Individual Study

1. As you begin each study, pray that God will speak to you through his Word.

2. Read the introduction to the study and respond to the personal reflection question or exercise. This is designed to help you focus on God and on the theme of the study.

3. Each study deals with a particular passage so that you can delve into the author's meaning in that context. Read and reread the passage to be studied. The questions are written using the language of the New International Version, so you may wish to use that version of the Bible. The New Revised Standard Version is also recommended.

4. This is an inductive Bible study, designed to help you discover for yourself what Scripture is saying. The study includes three types of questions. Observation questions ask about the basic facts: who, what, when, where and how. Interpretation questions delve into the meaning of the passage. Application questions help you discover the implications of the text for growing in Christ. These three keys unlock the treasures of Scripture.

Write your answers to the questions in the spaces provided or in a personal journal. Writing can bring clarity and deeper understanding of yourself and of God's Word.

5. It might be good to have a Bible dictionary handy. Use it to look up any unfamiliar words, names or places.

6. Use the prayer suggestion to guide you in thanking God for what you have learned and to pray about the applications that have come to mind.

7. You may want to go on to the suggestion under "Now or Later," or you may want to use that idea for your next study.

Suggestions for Members of a Group Study

1. Come to the study prepared. Follow the suggestions for individual study mentioned above. You will find that careful preparation will greatly enrich your time spent in group discussion.

2. Be willing to participate in the discussion. The leader of your group will not be lecturing. Instead, he or she will be encouraging the members of the group to discuss what they have learned. The leader will be asking the questions that are found in this guide.

3. Stick to the topic being discussed. Your answers should be based on the verses which are the focus of the discussion and not on outside authorities such as commentaries or speakers. These studies focus on a particular passage of Scripture. Only rarely should you refer to other portions of the Bible. This allows for everyone to participate in in-depth study on equal ground.

4. Be sensitive to the other members of the group. Listen attentively when they describe what they have learned. You may be surprised by their insights! Each question assumes a variety of answers. Many questions do not have "right" answers, particularly questions that aim at meaning or application. Instead the questions push us to explore the passage more thoroughly.

When possible, link what you say to the comments of others. Also, be affirming whenever you can. This will encourage some of the more hesitant members of the group to participate.

5. Be careful not to dominate the discussion. We are sometimes so eager to express our thoughts that we leave too little opportunity for others to respond. By all means participate! But allow others to also.

6. Expect God to teach you through the passage being discussed and through the other members of the group. Pray that you will have an enjoyable and profitable time together, but also that as a result of the study you will find ways that you can take action individually and/or as a group.

7. Remember that anything said in the group is considered confidential and should not be discussed outside the group unless specific permission is given to do so.

8. If you are the group leader, you will find additional suggestions at the back of the guide.

1

New Breath for Old Bones

Ezekiel 37:1-14

"Remember to breathe," said my friend as she consoled me. What strange advice. Isn't breathing one of those few things we aren't supposed to have to "remember" to do? In this instance, however, I had been grieving the sudden death of an old friend and was apparently in desperate need of such basic guidance. Grief and loss had nearly drained the life out of me. My insides felt withered and starved of essential nutrients. I was amazed by how a few deep breaths began to bring back the sensation of life. In this study we'll explore God's promise to send his own life-giving breath to renew our lives in a way we could never do for ourselves.

GROUP DISCUSSION. Describe a time when you could have used a reminder to breathe. What was happening in your life? Was someone there to help you?

PERSONAL REFLECTION. How do you experience the presence of God's Spirit in times of pain and loss?

The people of Israel lost their home to foreign invaders and were taken away as captives to a strange land. Overcome with grief, they wept aloud to the God who was supposed to look out for them. In response, the Spirit of the Lord came to the prophet Ezekiel and gave him a vision for the people. *Read Ezekiel 37:1-14.*

---

1. Imagine how Ezekiel must have felt after wandering back and forth through a valley full of old human bones. How does he respond to the Lord's surprising question in verse 3?

---

2. Notice that Ezekiel is not permitted to be a passive bystander in this vision. How did the Lord require Ezekiel to participate (v. 4)?

---

3. Why is it so important for the dry bones to "hear the word of the LORD" (v. 4)?

---

4. What prevents you from hearing God's Word in times of pain?

---

5. What happens as Ezekiel begins to prophesy as he is commanded (v. 7)?

6. Why are the bodies still lifeless after the bones come together and are covered with sinews and skin (v. 8)?

---

7. Why might the two-stage process of bringing these dead back to life mirror the two-stage creation of human beings in the very beginning (see Genesis 2:7)?

---

8. What do the bones (v. 11) and breath (v. 14) represent?

---

9. What did God promise the people through this vision (vv. 11-14)?

---

10. How does God's promise to raise up the dry bones and breathe new life into them give you courage in the face of pain and loss?

11. Who are the people in your life who feel that "hope is gone" (v. 11)?

12. How is God calling you to "prophesy" to the "bones" and "breath" today?

Give thanks to God that all hope is not lost, and pray that his Spirit would continue to breathe new life into you and all his people. Ask God to give you such confidence in his promises of resurrection and new creation that you joyfully speak this good news to all who are tempted to despair.

Now or Later

Ezekiel 37:1-14 is just one of several key Old Testament passages that began to cultivate a hope for resurrection among the people of Israel. Others you may want to reflect on are Job 19:25-27, Daniel 12:1-3, Isaiah 53:10-12 and Hosea 13:14. What images are used in each of these passages to communicate God's promises to his people? How do they find their ultimate fulfillment in Christ?

2

Healing and Restoration

Mark 5:21-43

"Take some extra vitamin C, drink this large glass of water and go back to bed!" Such was my mother's remedy for just about any sickness that dared inflict itself on me or my brother when we were kids. Only when things got desperate—totally beyond our control—would our family trouble a doctor or anyone else with our ailments. Most of the time we could handle it ourselves, thank you very much. Not only has this philosophy stayed with me as an adult, it has worked its way into other areas of my life as well. It is often very difficult for me to admit that something is out of my control. I'm embarrassed to cry out for help. But when I hit that point of desperation, when I realize that I simply don't have the personal resources to overcome a challenge, I reach out for others who do have the power to help me. In this study we'll meet two characters in desperate situations who take the risk of turning to someone more powerful than themselves for healing and restoration.

GROUP DISCUSSION. Describe a time when you felt overwhelmed by a problem and reached out to someone for help. How did you feel before you asked for help? How did you feel after? What was the result?

PERSONAL REFLECTION. In what circumstances is it difficult for you to trust in others to help you?

After leaving the Gentile region of the Decapolis, Jesus returns to Galilee to continue his ministry of teaching and healing. There he is met by a great crowd of people who are eager for his time and attention. *Read Mark 5:21-43.*

1. Imagine that you are in the crowd of people gathered around Jesus (v. 21), excited that such a great healer has come to your town. Would you try to approach him? If so, what kind of healing would you ask for?

2. In the midst of this needy multitude, one particularly desperate man makes his way to center stage. What does he ask of Jesus (v. 23)?

3. Jairus is identified as a synagogue leader. Why might it have been risky for him to throw himself at Jesus' feet and beg for help in public?

4. What risks do you need to take in order to turn to Jesus for help?

5. In verse 25, the scene is interrupted. The story of Jairus is suspended as yet another desperate character pushes her way into the picture. What do we learn about this unnamed woman (vv. 25-26)?

6. Why do you think the woman tried to get away with touching Jesus' cloak in secret (v. 28)?

---

7. When she touches Jesus' garment, the woman immediately knows that she is healed of her disease. But before she can run home rejoicing, Jesus calls her out: "Who touched my clothes?" (v. 30). Why do you think Jesus insisted on meeting the person who secretly sought healing from him?

---

8. Consider the kind words that Jesus speaks to the woman in verse 34. He calls her "daughter" and sends her home with a blessing of peace. What do we learn about the character of Jesus and the kind of healing he brings from this encounter?

---

9. In verse 35 the story of Jairus resumes with some devastating news: "Your daughter is dead." Jesus has taken too long to get there and now all hope is gone. How might Jairus have felt toward Jesus at this moment?

---

10. Jesus, however, is not discouraged by this news of the girl's death. What does Jesus mean when he tells the distraught people that "the child is not dead but asleep" (v. 39)?

11. Imagine yourself in this scene. What might it have been like to be among the people mourning the death of the girl at one moment and then "completely astonished" at the next?

What might it have been like to be the little girl who was brought back from death?

---

12. In both stories told here, desperate people reach out to Jesus, daring to trust in him as their last hope. As a result of their faith, we catch a glimpse of resurrection wholeness as Jesus brings healing and restoration right here in the midst of our world. Where do you see the healing and resurrection power of Jesus at work in your world?

Spend some time in praise and thanks to God for the healing and restoration that come through Jesus Christ. Offer prayers for specific needs in your life and those around you, daring to trust that God will demonstrate the power of the resurrection in your world today.

Now or Later

Mark's Gospel tells many stories of the healing and resurrection power of Jesus. For example, look at Mark 1:29-31; 1:40-42; 2:1-11; 3:1-6; 5:1-20; 7:31-37; 8:22-26. What do these stories have in common? What do we learn from them about Jesus, his concern for people, and the kind of healing and restoration that he brings?

3

A Love Stronger
Than Death

John 11:17-44

Boy and girl meet and fall in love. Someone puts an obstacle in the way of their love. Girl fakes her death to get around obstacle. Boy finds girl and thinks she's dead. Boy despairs and kills himself. Girl wakes up and finds boy dead. Girl despairs and kills herself.

Does this story sound familiar to you? Many of us would quickly identify it as (roughly) the plot of *Romeo and Juliet*. Indeed it is. But Shakespeare's story didn't come out of nowhere. Similar stories of passionate human love ending in tragedy and death have been quite common throughout history. There seems to be a widespread belief that love is powerful stuff—and potentially fatal! But in this study we'll discover another kind of love that is even stronger. And unlike the broken human love that can end in devastation and death, this love leads to resurrection and life.

GROUP DISCUSSION. What are some popular love stories from books, television, movies or real life? How do they reveal both the intensity and the brokenness of human love?

PERSONAL REFLECTION. How has human love brought both joy and pain to your life?

Jesus didn't show up. Mary and Martha called for him when their brother Lazarus grew very sick. They waited for him, but he didn't come. And then it was too late. But when Jesus finally does arrive on the scene, he demonstrates that his love for Lazarus is far greater than mere human love could ever be. *Read John 11:17-44.*

---

1. Many friends and relatives gathered around Mary and Martha to offer consolation (v. 19). If you had been there, what would you have said to these grief-stricken sisters?

---

2. How did Martha react when Jesus finally showed up (vv. 21-22)?

---

3. Jesus attempts to comfort Martha by assuring her that her brother will "rise again" (v. 23). How does Martha understand this promise?

---

4. What new perspective and promise does Jesus offer Martha in the midst of her grief (vv. 24-25)?

---

5. Think about how you would answer Jesus' question in verse 26. How does a person's answer to this question affect the way he or she responds to death?

6. How does Mary's reaction to Jesus (vv. 32-33) compare with Martha's?

---

7. This story emphasizes several times that Jesus is "deeply moved" and "troubled," even to the point of weeping (vv. 33-35, 38). How do those gathered around Jesus interpret his display of emotion (vv. 36-37)?

---

8. Earlier in John's Gospel, we are told that Jesus, God's only Son, has "made known" the Father to us (John 1:18). What in particular do Jesus' tears at Lazarus's grave make known to us about the Father?

---

9. How do Jesus' tears challenge your understanding of God?

---

10. Along with the others gathered around, Jesus offers words of hope and tears of solidarity. But that's not all he does. As the one who himself embodied resurrection and life (v. 25), Jesus was able to do much more than anyone could have ever expected that day. How does Martha's reaction to Jesus' request in verse 39 demonstrate that she had not totally grasped the meaning of her earlier conversation with Jesus (vv. 21-27)?

11. How do you sometimes fail to understand and embrace God's promises?

---

12. This story invites us to trust in the strength of God's love for us. Just as Jesus loved Lazarus (v. 36) and had the power to call him forth from the grave, so is his love for us much stronger than death. How does God's strong love enable you to live and love more fully today?

Rest quietly and gratefully for a minute in the strength of God's love for you. Hear Jesus' voice calling you forth from death into new life. Pray that his love will give you courage and strength to live more fully for him each day.

Now or Later

Take a few minutes to read and reflect on the follow-up episode in John 12:1-11. Here we see different responses to the life-giving love that Jesus demonstrated to Lazarus and his sisters. What characters are present in this scene (vv. 1-4, 9, 10)? How does each character (or group) respond to what Jesus has done? Who demonstrates true understanding? Who totally misses the point?

4

Broken Bread, Open Eyes

Luke 24:13-35

When I was a college student living thousands of miles from home, I would often become anxious and lonely when certain major holidays approached and I was faced yet again with the prospect of not being able to celebrate with my family. But then something quite remarkable would happen—various friends and professors would notice my predicament and take pity on me. They would invite me into their homes and give me a place at their dinner tables. Though I would walk through the door a total stranger to many who were gathered, something wonderful would happen as thanksgiving was offered, dishes were passed and the feasting began. Somehow by the end of the meal I would feel known, loved and accepted as part of the family—even if just for that one occasion. Meals shared in a spirit of love and friendship would often transform my holiday sadness into great laughter and joy. In this study we'll see how the risen Lord transformed a similar occasion.

GROUP DISCUSSION. What is one of your most memorable meals with friends or family?

PERSONAL REFLECTION. How have shared meals opened up new relationships or deepened existing relationships in your life?

On the day Jesus rose from the dead, two disheartened followers set out from Jerusalem to return to their home in Emmaus. Let's explore their encounter with the "stranger" along the way and see how it transformed their lives. *Read Luke 24:13-35.*

1. What mix of emotions might the two followers have been feeling as they began to make their way back to Emmaus?

2. How did the two followers initially respond to Jesus when he "came up and walked along with them" on the road (vv. 15-18)?

3. What might have kept them from understanding his true identity?

4. What keeps you from recognizing the presence of Jesus walking along the road with you in your life?

5. Verse 27 tells us that "beginning with Moses and all the Prophets, he explained to them what was said in all the Scriptures concerning himself." Why was it important for Jesus to explain from the Hebrew Scriptures his identity and all that had happened in recent days?

6. How does studying the Scriptures help prepare you to recognize the presence of Jesus in your life and in the world around you?

7. What does Jesus do after he sits down at the table with the two followers (v. 30)?

8. Why do you think their eyes are opened at this particular moment (v. 31)?

9. How does the risen Jesus still make himself known to us in the breaking of bread and sharing of meals?

10. Why is it significant that the two recall feeling as though their hearts were "burning" within them as they walked along the road with Jesus (v. 32)?

11. What did the two followers do when they returned to Jerusalem (v. 35)?

12. How might you help others recognize the presence of the risen Lord and invite them to share in all that he offers them?

Give thanks to God for walking with you in the midst of your particular struggles and revealing himself to you as the risen Lord. Pray that you might know him more deeply as you feast with him and are transformed by his presence, and that you might joyfully invite others to know him too.

Now or Later

Genesis 3:6-7 speaks of another incident where two people shared a meal and had their eyes opened. Scholars have suggested that Luke 24:30-31 is intended as a reversal of what happened in the Genesis 3 story. Read Genesis 3:1-19 and reflect on the "meal" described there and its consequences for humankind. Who offered Adam and Eve the food? What did they "know" or "recognize" once they ate of it? What impact did this have for them and all their future descendants? Then, by way of comparison, look again at Luke 24. Who offered the food? What did they "recognize"? What was the long-term impact? Spend some time reflecting on the ways the resurrection of Jesus reverses the fall of the first human couple and what that means for your life as a follower of the risen One.

5

A Mission with Promise

Matthew 28:1-10, 16-20

It's your first day at a new job. You arrive at the office expecting to have some time to settle into your cubicle, learn your way around and meet your coworkers. No such luck. Your boss has already assigned you a major project. As you look over the expectations, your heart rate rises. Panic sets in. You have no idea how to do this job. You begin to wonder if they've made a terrible mistake hiring you. You momentarily consider packing it in and heading home in quiet defeat.

But suddenly one of your new colleagues pokes her head in your office. She introduces herself and explains that she's worked at the company for many years. Seeing the fear in your eyes, she assures you that she knows well the pressures of your job. In fact, she had even served in that position herself for the past few years before being promoted to her current role. Then, totally unexpectedly, she volunteers to work alongside you this week to help you through your project. Your joy and relief are incalculable. Rather than dreading the week, you now look forward to it. The promised presence of a caring and experienced mentor makes all the difference. In this study, we'll see how the risen Christ goes before us and with us in his mission to the world.

GROUP DISCUSSION. Describe a time when a more experienced colleague, friend or mentor came alongside you to help you accomplish something. What did you learn from him or her?

PERSONAL REFLECTION. Who are the people in your life that have gone before you and walked alongside you? How has their guidance and presence made a difference?

Matthew's account of Jesus' crucifixion mentions the presence of many women who had followed Jesus from Galilee and provided for his needs in his most desperate hour (Mt 27:55). Among them were Mary Magdalene and Mary the mother of James and Joseph (v. 56), who stayed with Jesus until his body had been laid in the tomb. These two women returned to the tomb on Sunday morning and became the first of Jesus' followers to learn the incredible news. *Read Matthew 28:1-10.*

---

1. Notice how quickly this story progresses. In just the first six verses there is a rapid and radical change of circumstances. What unexpected events unfold before the eyes of the women in this opening scene (vv. 1-6)?

---

2. Why does the angel invite the women to "come and see the place where he lay" (v. 6)?

---

3. What message does the angel give the women to pass on to the rest of the disciples (v. 7)?

---

4. Why was it important for Jesus to go ahead of them to Galilee (v. 7)?

5. How has Jesus gone ahead of us as well?

6. What two ways do the women clearly demonstrate that they have believed the angel's message (vv. 8-9)?

7. Matthew doesn't actually give us a report of the women passing along the news of Jesus' resurrection to the other disciples, but this next scene implies that they did so. *Read Matthew 28:16-20.* Why is there a split reaction among the disciples when Jesus comes to them (v. 17)?

8. In what ways do you sometimes hesitate to respond to the risen Lord?

9. What threefold mission does Jesus give his disciples (vv. 19-20)?

10. How are you called to participate in this mission today?

---

11. What two promises does Jesus give his disciples as they carry out his mission (vv. 18, 20)?

---

12. What difference do these promises make as you take your place in Christ's mission?

Give thanks and celebrate the Lord's promise to be with you until the end of the age. Ask that he reveal to you what role you can play in the work of speaking the good news of his resurrection and inviting others to follow him where he leads.

Now or Later

Matthew's Gospel locates some of Jesus' most important moments on mountains. For instance, read and reflect on a few of these: the third temptation (Mt 4:8-10), the Sermon on the Mount (Mt 5–7), Jesus' solitude (Mt 14:23), the transfiguration (Mt 17:1-6), and the final teaching on the Mount of Olives (Mt 24). How does Matthew 28:16-20 function as the grand finale to all of these mountain moments? How does each mountain moment find its fulfillment in this climatic interaction between the risen Lord and his followers? How do they make sense only in light of the resurrection? How do they help us understand what it means to participate in the mission of Christ?

6

Bold Allegiance

My parents met and married in San Diego in 1969, the year the Padres were founded as a Major League Baseball team. They caught the spirit of the team from the beginning and haven't looked back. Their loyalty keeps them attending games now well into their retirement—still decked out in their Padres shirts, boldly letting the world know whose side they're on no matter the odds against them. In this study we will reflect on the beginning of something much greater. We'll be invited to radical devotion and bold allegiance to One who is supremely worthy. And unlike our favorite sports teams, this One will never disappoint us.

GROUP DISCUSSION. How do you publically demonstrate your association with a favorite team or organization?

PERSONAL REFLECTION. What are you most deeply devoted to? How do you act on this devotion?

On the day of Pentecost the Holy Spirit came with great power on the disciples of the risen and ascended Jesus. In response to the confusion and outright mockery of those who observed, Peter boldly testified that the promises of God had been fulfilled. *Read Acts 2:22-36.*

1. If you had been in the crowd of Israelites that day, what overall effect do you think Peter's speech would have had on you?

---

2. What serious accusation does Peter bring against the gathered Israelites (vv. 22-23)?

---

3. Why was it "impossible" for Jesus to be held in the power of death (vv. 24-28)?

---

4. What Scriptures does Peter base his message on (vv. 25-28, 34-35)?

---

5. What central point does Peter make by quoting these particular Scriptures (vv. 29-31, 34-36)?

---

6. In verse 32 Peter describes himself and the other apostles as "witnesses" of the risen Jesus. What does it mean to be a witness?

---

7. How are you also a witness to the risen Lord?

8. After he was raised, Jesus was exalted to the right hand of the Father. What gift did he receive from the Father that he graciously passed along to his people (v. 33)?

_____

9. How has this gift helped you as a follower of Jesus?

_____

10. Why does Peter insist that Jesus is "both Lord and Messiah" (v. 36)?

_____

11. What difference does Jesus' exaltation as the true Lord of all make in your own life?

_____

12. How does your allegiance to Jesus as King, like Peter, give you confidence to bear witness to him?

Give thanks to God for forming a community of faithful witnesses who declare their allegiance to the true Lord and King of all. Ask God to strengthen you to be part of that faithful community so that you may boldly testify to the risen Christ everywhere you go.

Now or Later

Reflect prayerfully on Psalm 16 and Psalm 110. What does each of them teach about the faithful rule of God? How do they help you understand what it means to live as a subject of God's kingdom in Christ?

7

A Meaningful Life

1 Corinthians 15:35-58

A few years ago I read a fascinating study about caterpillars and butterflies. Scientists have long marveled at the metamorphosis these creatures undergo—at the way their entire substance seems to break down and form into something totally new. This particular study discovered that caterpillars that were trained to avoid certain smells retained that training even after their complete transformation into butterflies. In other words, the caterpillars gained experience and formed habits that had enduring value. What happened to them in their immature state was meaningful for their life as mature creatures. In this study we'll discover that in the resurrection the same is true for us.

GROUP DISCUSSION. Describe an event or experience from your childhood that continues to shape who you are as an adult today.

PERSONAL REFLECTION. What have been some of the most meaningful experiences of your life? How would you be a different person without them?

The apostle Paul begins his extended reflection in 1 Corinthians 15 on the significance of Christ's resurrection by recounting the tradition about the bodily resurrection of Jesus that had been passed down through those like himself who personally encountered the risen Christ (vv. 3-11). He then addresses a number of questions and misunderstandings that had arisen in the Corinthian church about the implications of Christ's resurrection for the rest of us. *Read 1 Corinthians 15:35-58.*

---

1. We get the sense from verse 35 that some of the Corinthian believers were struggling to wrap their minds around Christian teaching about life after death. When you picture the afterlife, what do you see?

---

2. What three analogies from the natural world does Paul use to help us understand about various types of bodies (vv. 36-41)?

---

3. What is the main point of each of these analogies?

---

4. Paul contrasts two types of bodies in particular: "natural" and "spiritual." What are the characteristics of each type of body (vv. 42-44)?

---

5. What is the point of Paul's comparison of the "first Adam" and the "last Adam" (vv. 45-50)?

6. What "mystery" is revealed in verses 51-53?

---

7. How does this mystery bring about the fulfillment of the saying, "Death has been swallowed up in victory" (v. 54)?

---

8. Paul bursts into praise of God (v. 57) after contemplating this mystery. How do you react to this mystery after reflecting on it?

---

9. What overall conclusion does Paul draw from this discussion of resurrection (v. 58)?

---

10. Why does Paul draw a conclusion focused on this present world when his whole discussion has been oriented toward the future?

---

11. Why is our work in the Lord "not in vain" (v. 58)?

12. How might you devote yourself more fully to your own "work of the Lord" (v. 58)?

As you reflect on the great mystery of transformation, offer praise to God who gives you victory over death through Jesus Christ your Lord. Ask God to strengthen you to devote yourself fully to the work of the Lord that will never fade away.

Now or Later

It can be a bit mind bending to ponder what life will be like in a transformed body. Since Jesus Christ is the only one so far who has gone through this human metamorphosis, it's worth exploring what we know of his post-resurrection experience. Read and reflect on John 20–21. What similarities do you see in how Jesus looks, behaves and interacts with others as the risen Lord compared with before he died? What differences do you see? How do these post-resurrection stories of Jesus help shape the way you understand your own future and the future of God's world?

8

Freedom to Live

Shouts of "freedom!" and "we're free!" echoed through the hallways and across the schoolyard. It was as though the shackles of their public school education had been loosed and the prison doors of their class-rooms thrown wide open. The wondrous glory of summer vacation re-flected off their faces in great gap-toothed grins. Of course, as second graders, they were far too young to understand the long-term benefits of education. All they knew in this moment was that life would be different for the next two and a half months, and they couldn't wait to embrace all it had to offer. In this study, we'll explore the kind of freedom we experi-ence through Christ's resurrection.

GROUP DISCUSSION. What are some common uses of the term *freedom* in today's world?

PERSONAL REFLECTION. When in your life have you felt truly free? What emotions or actions accompanied your sense of freedom?

After describing in detail the sad state of humankind in captivity to sin and death (Romans 7), the apostle Paul looks to the Spirit who raised Christ from the dead for hope in an otherwise hopeless situa-tion. *Read Romans 8:1-11.*

1. How would you define or describe the nature of true freedom?

_____

2. What assurance is offered in verse 1 to those who are in Christ Jesus?

_____

3. In what way has the Spirit of life set us free from sin and death (vv. 2-4)?

_____

4. What does the Spirit desire and what does the flesh desire (v. 5)?

_____

5. What does it look like for us to "live in accordance with the Spirit" in everyday life (v. 5)?

_____

6. What comes to those who set their mind on the Spirit instead of the flesh (v. 6)?

_____

7. If we are Christ's people who live in the Spirit, why do we sometimes still experience the hostility of the flesh toward God (vv. 7-8)?

8. In what areas of your life do you seek freedom from the flesh in order to live for God?

---

9. In what way are our bodies already dead (v. 10)?

---

10. The very same Spirit who raised Jesus from the dead lives in us. According to verse 11, what is this Spirit doing for us?

---

11. Where do you see the Spirit of the risen Lord at work in your own life?

---

12. How might you more fully embrace the freedom of the Spirit?

Celebrate that you are no longer condemned for your sins and failures. Rejoice in your freedom from captivity to sin and death through the Spirit of the risen Lord. Ask God to help you live more fully in step with the Spirit of resurrection at work in you so you may experience his life and peace more each day.

Now or Later

The nature of true Christian freedom seems to have been one of Paul's favorite subjects. Reflect on Romans 6, Galatians 5 and 2 Corinthians 3. How does the biblical understanding of freedom compare with popular notions of freedom? What role does the Spirit play? Why does the resurrection matter?

9

New Clothes

Colossians 3:1-17

It didn't take her long to realize that she was terribly underdressed. This was her first time at one of her new acquaintance's garden parties and she had gravely misjudged the dress code. Never before had she noticed just how ragged her favorite jeans were. Or how obvious that stain on her blouse was. And why did she opt for the flip-flops—today of all days? As the other attendees began glancing skeptically in her direction, she wished she could vanish and reenter the party wearing the proper attire. In this study we'll get a "fashion lesson" from the apostle Paul, who instructs us what not to wear in the presence of the risen Lord and offers us a much better wardrobe instead.

GROUP DISCUSSION. Describe a time when you were either embarrassed by what you were wearing or felt that your clothing gave a wrong impression of you. Did this experience change the way you dressed in the future?

PERSONAL REFLECTION. How do your actions function as "clothing" in the way they reveal to others something about who you are or what you value?

The Colossian believers were struggling to understand how to live as Christians. Some were even turning back to various human traditions and philosophies (2:8) or rules and observances (2:16) for guidance. So Paul explains the unique nature of the Christian life to them in terms of what it means for believers to be included in the risen and exalted life of Christ. Then he invites them to strip off their old clothes and put on some new ones. *Read Colossians 3:1-17.*

1. In what ways do you share the Colossians' struggle with knowing how to live as a Christian in a not-so-Christian world?

2. How do verses 1-4 challenge and reorient the way you understand who you are as a Christian?

3. What are the "things above" that we are instructed to set our hearts and minds on (vv. 1-2)?

4. What will happen to us when Christ "appears" (v. 4)?

5. What are some of the earthly things that we are instructed to "put to death" or "rid ourselves of" (vv. 5-9)?

6. Why must we strip off these earthly things?

_____

7. What earthly things do you most struggle to get rid of in your life?

_____

8. What are some of the wide-reaching, society-altering benefits of being clothed with the new self (vv. 10-11)?

_____

9. How is our new clothing characterized (vv. 12-14)?

_____

10. Why do we often have a difficult time wearing some of these new items?

_____

11. How does Paul encourage us to draw on Christ's own resources as we clothe ourselves (see particularly vv. 13, 15, 16)?

12. How would your life look different if every "word" and "deed"
were done in the name of the risen Lord and with gratitude to God
(v. 17)?

*Give thanks to the Lord for the great riches that are yours in the risen
Christ. Express your desire to be finished with the tattered sin-stained
clothing of your old self and be fully adorned with the beautiful garments
of the new self, reflecting the glory of Christ in all things.*

Now or Later

The image of putting off the old self and "clothing" ourselves with
something new is a common image in the New Testament. Take some
time to read and reflect on Ephesians 4:22-25, 1 Peter 5:5-6 and Revelation 3:17-18. What specifically do each of these passages ask us to
put aside? What new clothing do they encourage us to put on? How
do the characteristics of the new clothing reflect the character of
Christ himself?

10

All Things New

I'm always inspired by artists who take old, worn out, broken items and make them into something beautiful and new. Collages made from scraps of paper. Sculptures made from the remains of aluminum cans. Wallets made from old clothes and rags. I've even seen lovely purses made from gum wrappers. Things that look to most of us as though they have no further purpose in this world are refashioned and given a new future. Perhaps this is a little bit like God's intention for our world. In this study we'll watch with John as a new future for God's resurrected people is fashioned out of the brokenness of this world.

GROUP DISCUSSION. When have you seen someone take something old and apparently useless and make it into something new?

PERSONAL REFLECTION. What feels broken and worn out in your life? In what areas do you long to be made new and given new direction and purpose?

Much of the wild, apocalyptic book of Revelation is concerned with the brokenness of the world and the dire consequences of evil and rebellion against God. But it also assures us that God has not abandoned the world. It promises that death will be cast out and the whole creation be renewed by the power of the one who triumphed over the grave. There is an unimaginably beautiful future in store for the resurrected people of God. *Read Revelation 21:1-8.*

---

1. Imagine that you are with John watching this vision unfold before you. How would you respond to each of the images?

---

2. What happens to the first heaven and the first earth that we live in now (v. 1)?

---

3. Why do you think this must this happen?

---

4. The voice from the throne declares that "God's dwelling place is now among the people" (v. 3). How will this be different from the way we experience God's presence with us now?

---

5. What will life be like in this place (v. 4)?

6. Perhaps the most striking promise is that death itself "will be no more" (v. 4). How does the work of Jesus Christ, the Lamb who sits on the throne in Revelation, ensure that this promise will be fulfilled?

_____

7. What is included in the "everything" that will be made new (v. 5)?

_____

8. What gift is promised to those who are thirsty (v. 6)?

_____

9. What do you thirst for?

_____

10. How do we achieve victory in order to inherit this brand new creation (v. 7)?

_____

11. Why will some people be kept out of the new creation (v. 8)?

12. How might this vision of a death-free future—where all creation is healed from its hurts and made beautiful and new—shape the way you live today?

Give thanks to God that death's days are numbered. Marvel before him at the great work of resurrection and transformation that he has already begun in Jesus Christ and will one day carry to completion. Pray that you will learn to live each day as a new creature, as one who reflects the beauty of the world to come right in the midst of the present time.

Now or Later

The vision of the new heavens and new earth reflected here in Revelation 21 comes straight from the Hebrew prophets. For instance, read and reflect on Isaiah 65:13-25 and 66:10-24. Do some of these images sound familiar? How does the vision offered in Isaiah help complete the picture of the new heavens and new earth that we glimpse in Revelation 21? What hope do these passages offer to the world? What warning do they bring?

Leader's Notes

MY GRACE IS SUFFICIENT FOR YOU. (2 COR 12:9)

Leading a Bible discussion can be an enjoyable and rewarding experience. But it can also be *scary*—especially if you've never done it before. If this is your feeling, you're in good company. When God asked Moses to lead the Israelites out of Egypt, he replied, "O Lord, please send someone else to do it!" (Ex 4:13). It was the same with Solomon, Jeremiah and Timothy, but God helped these people in spite of their weaknesses, and he will help you as well.

You don't need to be an expert on the Bible or a trained teacher to lead a Bible discussion. The idea behind these inductive studies is that the leader guides group members to discover for themselves what the Bible has to say. This method of learning will allow group members to remember much more of what is said than a lecture would.

These studies are designed to be led easily. As a matter of fact, the flow of questions through the passage from observation to interpretation to application is so natural that you may feel that the studies lead themselves. This study guide is also flexible. You can use it with a variety of groups—student, professional, neighborhood or church groups. Each study takes forty-five to sixty minutes in a group setting.

There are some important facts to know about group dynamics and encouraging discussion. The suggestions listed below should enable you to effectively and enjoyably fulfill your role as leader.

Preparing for the Study

1. Ask God to help you understand and apply the passage in your own life. Unless this happens, you will not be prepared to lead others. Pray too for the various members of the group. Ask God to open your hearts to the message of his Word and motivate you to action.

2. Read the introduction to the entire guide to get an overview of the entire book and the issues which will be explored.

3. As you begin each study, read and reread the assigned Bible passage to familiarize yourself with it.

4. This study guide is based on the New International Version of the Bible. It will help you and the group if you use this translation as the basis for your study and discussion.

5. Carefully work through each question in the study. Spend time in meditation and reflection as you consider how to respond.

6. Write your thoughts and responses in the space provided in the study guide. This will help you to express your understanding of the passage clearly.

7. It might help to have a Bible dictionary handy. Use it to look up any unfamiliar words, names or places. (For additional help on how to study a passage, see chapter five of *How to Lead a LifeGuide Bible Study,* InterVarsity Press.)

8. Consider how you can apply the Scripture to your life. Remember that the group will follow your lead in responding to the studies. They will not go any deeper than you do.

9. Once you have finished your own study of the passage, familiarize yourself with the leader's notes for the study you are leading. These are designed to help you in several ways. First, they tell you the purpose the study guide author had in mind when writing the study. Take time to think through how the study questions work together to accomplish that purpose. Second, the notes provide you with additional background information or suggestions on group dynamics for various questions. This information can be useful when people have difficulty understanding or answering a question. Third, the leader's notes can alert you to potential problems you may encounter during the study.

10. If you wish to remind yourself of anything mentioned in the leader's notes, make a note to yourself below that question in the study.

Leading the Study

1. Begin the study on time. Open with prayer, asking God to help the group to understand and apply the passage.

2. Be sure that everyone in your group has a study guide. Encourage the group to prepare beforehand for each discussion by reading the introduction to the guide and by working through the questions in the study.

3. At the beginning of your first time together, explain that these studies are meant to be discussions, not lectures. Encourage the members of the group to participate. However, do not put pressure on those who may be hesitant to speak during the first few sessions. You may want to suggest the following guidelines to your group.

☐ Stick tó the topic being discussed.

☐ Your responses should be based on the verses which are the focus of the discussion and not on outside authorities such as commentaries or speakers.

☐ These studies focus on a particular passage of Scripture. Only rarely should you refer to other portions of the Bible. This allows for everyone to participate in in-depth study on equal ground.

☐ Anything said in the group is considered confidential and will not be discussed outside the group unless specific permission is given to do so.

☐ We will listen attentively to each other and provide time for each person present to talk.

☐ We will pray for each other.

4. Have a group member read the introduction at the beginning of the discussion.

5. Every session begins with a group discussion question. The question or activity is meant to be used before the passage is read. The question introduces the theme of the study and encourages group members to begin to open up. Encourage as many members as possible to participate, and be ready to get the discussion going with your own response.

This section is designed to reveal where our thoughts or feelings need to be transformed by Scripture. That is why it is especially important not to read the passage before the discussion question is asked. The passage will tend to color the honest reactions people would otherwise give because they are, of course, supposed to think the way the Bible does.

You may want to supplement the group discussion question with an icebreaker to help people to get comfortable. See the community section of *Small Group Idea Book* for more ideas.

You also might want to use the personal reflection question with your group. Either allow a time of silence for people to respond individually or discuss it together.

6. Have a group member (or members if the passage is long) read aloud the passage to be studied. Then give people several minutes to read the passage again silently so that they can take it all in.

7. Question 1 will generally be an overview question designed to briefly survey the passage. Encourage the group to look at the whole passage, but try to avoid getting sidetracked by questions or issues that will be addressed later in the study.

8. As you ask the questions, keep in mind that they are designed to be used just as they are written. You may simply read them aloud. Or you may prefer to express them in your own words.

There may be times when it is appropriate to deviate from the study guide. For example, a question may have already been answered. If so, move on to the next question. Or someone may raise an important question not covered in the guide. Take time to discuss it, but try to keep the group from going off on tangents.

9. Avoid answering your own questions. If necessary, repeat or rephrase them until they are clearly understood. Or point out something you read in the leader's notes to clarify the context or meaning. An eager group quickly becomes passive and silent if they think the leader will do most of the talking.

10. Don't be afraid of silence. People may need time to think about the question before formulating their answers.

11. Don't be content with just one answer. Ask, "What do the rest of you think?" or "Anything else?" until several people have given answers to the question.

12. Acknowledge all contributions. Try to be affirming whenever possible. Never reject an answer. If it is clearly off-base, ask, "Which verse led you to that conclusion?" or again, "What do the rest of you think?"

13. Don't expect every answer to be addressed to you, even though this will probably happen at first. As group members become more at ease, they will begin to truly interact with each other. This is one sign of healthy discussion.

14. Don't be afraid of controversy. It can be very stimulating. If you don't resolve an issue completely, don't be frustrated. Move on and keep it in mind for later. A subsequent study may solve the problem.

15. Periodically summarize what the group has said about the passage. This helps to draw together the various ideas mentioned and gives continuity to the study. But don't preach.

16. At the end of the Bible discussion you may want to allow group members a time of quiet to work on an idea under "Now or Later." Then discuss what you experienced. Or you may want to encourage group members to work on these ideas between meetings. Give an opportunity during the session for people to talk about what they are learning.

17. Conclude your time together with conversational prayer, adapting the prayer suggestion at the end of the study to your group. Ask for God's help in following through on the commitments you've made.

18. End on time.

Many more suggestions and helps are found in *How to Lead a LifeGuide Bible Study.*

Components of Small Groups

A healthy small group should do more than study the Bible. There are four components to consider as you structure your time together.

Nurture. Small groups help us to grow in our knowledge and love of God. Bible study is the key to making this happen and is the foundation of your small group.

Community. Small groups are a great place to develop deep friendships with other Christians. Allow time for informal interaction before and after each study. Plan activities and games that will help you get to know each other. Spend time having fun together going on a picnic or cooking dinner together.

Worship and prayer. Your study will be enhanced by spending time praising God together in prayer or song. Pray for each other's needs and keep track of how God is answering prayer in your group. Ask God to help you to apply what you are learning in your study.

Outreach. Reaching out to others can be a practical way of applying what you are learning, and it will keep your group from becoming self-focused. Host a series of evangelistic discussions for your friends or neighbors. Clean up the yard of an elderly friend. Serve at a soup kitchen together, or spend a day working on a Habitat house.

Many more suggestions and helps in each of these areas are found in *Small Group Idea Book.* Information on building a small group can be found in *Small Group Leaders' Handbook* and *The Big Book on Small Groups* (both from InterVarsity Press). Reading through one of these books would be worth your time.

Study 1. New Breath for Old Bones. Ezekiel 37:1-14.

Purpose: To discover hope in the promise of a new beginning here and now.

Question 1. Participants may sympathize with Ezekiel's response: "Sovereign LORD, you alone know." Indeed! How are we supposed to know? From a human standpoint, bodies that have died and decayed certainly cannot live again. Yet rather than responding "Not a chance!" the prophet lets God have the final say on the matter. Apparent hopelessness is not necessarily *ultimate* hopelessness. Our perspective is limited.

Question 3. A related question here is: How are these old, dead bones supposed to "hear" anything? I love how Christopher J. H. Wright puts this problem: "Now it is a well-attested anatomical fact that although ears have many bones, bones do not have any ears. To preach to bones is even more futile than preaching to the deaf" (*The Message of Ezekiel*, Bible Speaks Today [Downers Grove, IL: InterVarsity Press, 2001], p. 306). But this is just the point. The people of Israel had been "deaf" to God's promises and had therefore given themselves up for dead. They desperately needed to hear again that God was still their God, to know that their future was full of hope and life.

Question 7. This question tries to get at the theological message of this passage. The account of the creation of the first human begins with the Lord forming Adam from the "dust of the ground" and "breathed into his nostrils the breath of life" (Gen 2:7). The message of Ezekiel's vision is nothing less than the promise of new creation. The same God who created the people of Israel in the first place would create them all over again from the dust of their dried-up bones. And just as the original humans were given a place to live and work and flourish, so the people of Israel would be restored to their land. It will be a brand new beginning.

Question 9. This vision uses the imagery of resurrection and new creation to speak of God's promise to restore Israel to their homeland. It represents the promise of forgiveness of past sins and the chance for a new start. It speaks of a hopeful future for a people who feared they had lost all hope.

Question 11. Encourage participants to be specific here. It's easy enough to say "the poor" or "the sick," but often challenging to name those particular people in our lives who badly need to "hear the word of the Lord."

Question 12. If you meet resistance to the idea that we "regular people" are called to "prophesy," you may want to talk about how *prophesy* in this context is simply another way of talking about "proclamation." We are all called to proclaim the good news to one another. And we are all called to pray for God's Spirit to come and renew this world, breathing new life into all who have given themselves up for dead.

Study 2. Healing and Restoration. Mark 5:21-43.

Purpose: To understand how those who dare to trust in Jesus find full healing and restoration.

Question 1. The aim of this question is to help participants place themselves in the story as those in need of Jesus' healing. You may need to remind your group that healing is not restricted to physical sickness but applies to emotional, psychological and relational brokenness as well. If some participants respond that they would hesitate to approach Jesus, ask what specifically would hold them back.

Question 3. In Mark 3:1-6, Jesus had greatly upset the religious leaders by healing a man on the sabbath day—to the point where they began to conspire to kill him. Jesus was not exactly an esteemed person in the eyes of the religious leaders! It's possible that Jairus was risking his own position in the synagogue by associating with Jesus. Certainly he must have been risking the anger of his colleagues by perhaps appearing to give Jesus a stamp of approval from the synagogue. By approaching Jesus in front of so many people, Jairus demonstrates not only the desperation of his situation but also his tremendous faith in Jesus' power. It was worth the risk to him.

Question 5. Important details to highlight include: (1) The woman had been suffering from a bleeding disorder (probably related to her menstrual cycle) for twelve years. (2) She had been through all kinds of different treatments under the care of many different doctors. (3) She was penniless as a result of spending so much trying to get better. (4) Her condition was now worse than ever. The main point: This is a desperate situation—one that may even resonate with participants in your group!

Question 6. A number of insightful responses might be offered here. Perhaps the woman didn't want to take up any of the great healer's time. Perhaps she was embarrassed by her condition and didn't want to have to explain it in front of Jesus and all the people. To these kinds of responses, you might add some biblical and historical context: A woman in this condition would have been considered unclean by Jewish law. Leviticus 15:19-30 speaks of the ritual impurity of woman during the days of their menstrual cycle: "When a woman has her regular flow of blood, the impurity of her monthly period will last seven days, and anyone who touches her will be unclean till evening" (Lev 15:19). It goes on to say that if a woman's bleeding extends beyond the normal seven-day period, then "she will be unclean as long as she has the discharge" (Lev 15:25). The woman knew that Jesus could not touch her without becoming unclean himself—perhaps she worried that he would not want to help her for this reason. Perhaps she worried about being scolded or condemned for being out in public where she might expose others to uncleanness.

Question 7. It's quite remarkable that Jesus took the time to make a personal connection with this woman—especially when he was in the midst of urgent business for a prominent leader. Clearly the healing and wholeness Jesus brings are not reserved for a certain class of people. It's possible Jesus wanted to address this woman personally because he knew that she needed more than physical healing. She had been separated from the community for over a decade. She was in desperate need of being embraced by others and reintegrated into society. Jesus saw a deeper need and took the opportunity to make the public aware that this woman's "hopeless" situation had changed.

Question 8. Our English translations usually render the Greek *eirene* as "peace," but it's likely that Jesus was giving the woman the traditional Hebrew blessing of *shalom* which goes beyond the simple feeling of tranquility to a renewed state of wholeness, health and rest. Calling the woman "daughter" would have pointed to her reintegration into family life and society. Many answers might be offered to this question of what we learn about Jesus from this, but his compassion and concern that the woman experience com-

plete healing and restoration in *every* area of her life should be highlighted.
Question 10. This is a confusing line. Did Jesus really believe the girl was
only sleeping? It's more likely that Jesus was making an important theological statement here. Because of the resurrection power he holds, death is no
more of a threat than simply falling asleep. It is only temporary. Jesus holds
the power of eternal life and will raise up those who have died as though
they had only drifted off for a short nap.

Study 3. A Love Stronger Than Death. John 11:17-44.
Purpose: To look to Jesus as the one whose strong love reaches beyond the grave.
Question 1. You might encourage participants to reflect on similar sce-
narios that they've experienced—funerals and times of mourning—and to
remember all the different emotions displayed and words spoken. What is
helpful to say? What is not helpful?
Question 3. Martha's interpretation of Jesus' words makes sense given the
typical Jewish understanding of resurrection in that time. Many believed
(based on passages such as Dan 12:2-3) that on the last day, God would call
forth his people from their graves, reawakening them for everlasting life. She
seems to have assumed that this was precisely the hope that Jesus was offer-
ing her. But Jesus was doing much more. He was transforming this hope. He
was recentering the promise of everlasting life around himself and moving its
fulfillment forward to the present time.
Question 5. This is an important question to consider when wrestling with
the overall theological message of this story. Jesus reconfigures the meaning
of life and death by placing himself at the center: "I am the resurrection and
the life." To really believe this is to entrust ourselves entirely to him. To set
aside a self-centered life for the sake of something so much better. To find
hope and assurance even in the face of death. The first question of the Hei-
delberg Catechism asks, "What is your only comfort in life and in death?"
The response reflects precisely the kind of faith Jesus asks of us in light of
his claim to be the resurrection and the life: "That I belong—body and soul,
in life and in death—not to myself but to my faithful Savior, Jesus Christ."
Questions 8-9. Nobody explains this better than N. T. Wright: "When we
look at Jesus, not least when we look at Jesus in tears, we are seeing not just a
flesh-and-blood human being but the Word made flesh (Jn 1:1-14). The Word,
through whom the worlds were made, weeps like a baby at the grave of his
friend. Only when we stop and ponder this will we understand the full mystery
of John's Gospel. Only when we put away our high-and-dry pictures of who God
is and replace them with pictures in which the Word who is God can cry with

the world's crying will we discover what the word 'God' really means" (*John for Everyone: Part Two* [Louisville, KY: Westminster John Knox, 2002], pp. 10-11). **Questions 10-11.** Martha's gut reaction was to protest Jesus' request that the stone be moved. Why would he want to do that? The body is going to stink! Martha's theology simply hasn't caught up with Jesus yet. Even though Jesus had taken the time to explain that everything was different now that he had come, she had not internalized his words or applied them to the current situation. Participants may resonate with this experience greatly—I certainly do! I may understand and genuinely believe that God is both loving and powerful, but I lag behind when it comes to actually trusting God to be loving and powerful in my life. Encourage participants to share some concrete examples.

Study 4. Broken Bread, Open Eyes. Luke 24:13-35.
Purpose: To learn to look for the risen Lord to make himself known in the breaking of bread.
Question 2. The two followers totally miss the fact that Jesus is with them. They take him for a mere stranger—and a completely clueless one at that! They couldn't have been more wrong.
Question 3. Participants may begin to speculate about the nature of Jesus' resurrection body and wonder if the disciples didn't recognize him because he looked so different. While this is possible, perhaps the real point is that these two heartbroken people did not have eyes to see Jesus walking right next to them. To them, he was gone. They were blinded by their grief, disappointment and failure to understand God's redemptive purposes.
Question 4. Many of us are able to sympathize with these two. Weighed down by the cares, fears and disappointments of our lives and the world around us, our eyes grow dim and we lose focus. We stop expecting God to be there, so we stop looking for him. Encourage participants to name specific worries or fears (related to family, finances, health, etc.) and articulate how these prevent them from seeing the risen Lord walking alongside them.
Question 5. While we don't know much about these two followers, it's likely that they were faithful Jewish believers, looking and longing for their God to come through on his promises to Israel. Their hope was in the Hebrew Scriptures (our Old Testament), but they needed help understanding how these Scriptures had always pointed toward events happening right before their eyes in Jesus' life, death, resurrection and exaltation.
Question 6. Encourage concrete examples here. Perhaps, for instance, someone read Psalm 19:1 ("the heavens declare the glory of God") and then was amazed when she looked up and noticed how the mountains just

outside her window so clearly testify to God's greatness.

Questions 7-8. What's particularly interesting here is that Jesus, the guest, suddenly assumes the role of the host. He takes the bread, blesses it, breaks it and gives it. Notice the similarities between this language and Luke's depiction of the Lord's Supper in Luke 22:19. Because in sharing bread Jesus essentially shares *himself,* this is the moment when they recognize him.

Question 9. This question tries to get at the heart of what this passage has to teach us about the resurrection. The ultimate response, of course, is that Jesus meets us this way when the Christian community gathers to celebrate the Lord's Supper. But there are other ways too. Table fellowship is a major theme in Luke's Gospel: Jesus is always eating with people! Perhaps as we share meals—extending and receiving hospitality—with friends and enemies alike, we will find our own eyes opened to the presence of the risen Lord in our midst.

Question 10. As the two followers reflected on their experience with Jesus that day, they were probably astounded that they hadn't put it together. Of course that was Jesus walking with them! He had been there all along. This highlights what Fred Craddock calls the "central role of memory in faith and understanding"—often we don't understand what's happening as it's happening, but once our eyes have been opened we are able to see into our past and interpret more accurately what was happening (see Fred B. Craddock, *Luke,* Interpretation [Louisville, KY: Westminster John Knox, 1990]).

Now or Later. Luke 24:31-32 may be understood as a reversal—as the ultimate "undoing"—of what happened when Adam and Eve ate of the forbidden fruit. N. T. Wright is particularly helpful on this point:

> The first meal mentioned in the Bible is the moment when Adam and Eve eat the forbidden fruit. The direct result is new and unwelcome knowledge: "the eyes of them both were opened, and they knew that they were naked." . . . Now this other couple . . . are at table, and are confronted with new and deeply welcome knowledge: "their eyes were opened and they recognized him." . . . This, Luke is saying, is the ultimate redemption; this is the meal which signifies that the long exile of the human race, not just of Israel, is now over at last. (N. T. Wright, *Resurrection of the Son of God* [Minneapolis: Fortress, 2003], p. 652)

Study 5. A Mission with Promise. Matthew 28:1-10, 16-20.

Purpose: To respond to the call to participate in the mission of the risen Lord.

Question 2. It might be helpful to point out that these were the same women who saw where the body was laid in Matthew 27:60-61. They were not mistaken about the place. To enter the tomb and see for themselves that the body was no longer where they saw it previously would add credibility to the angel's message and thus to the report the women passed along to the others. In fact, this seems to be the only reason the tomb is opened at all here. R. T. France has observed, "There is no suggestion that the opening of the tomb is necessary to allow the risen Christ to come out; indeed in v. 6 it is clear that he has already risen. The women are called not to see him rising . . . but to see that he has risen; the opening of the tomb is thus for their benefit, not for his" (*Matthew*, Tyndale New Testament Commentary [Downers Grove, IL: IVP Academic, 2008], p. 412).

Question 4. Perhaps most significantly, in Matthew 26:32 Jesus had promised to go before his disciples to Galilee after he was raised from the dead. There may also be some significance that the risen Jesus leaves the city where he was opposed and crucified by the Jewish people to meet his disciples in the place Matthew identified earlier (in Mt 4:15) as "Galilee of the Gentiles" for his final teaching and commissioning. This may underscore God's plan to bring restoration and healing to all the world.

Question 5. This question intends to help participants consider the broader theological significance of the passage. On the surface there may not seem to be much significance to the idea that Jesus "goes ahead" of the disciples. But in a passage about resurrection, it's worth considering what may be happening beneath the surface. Indeed, Jesus has gone ahead of us through death and into God's new creation. Through him God's future has broken into our present reality. And the risen Lord has also gone ahead of us in the mission to spread the word and invite all nations into this wonderful new reality (Mt 28:19).

Question 6. First, the women "run" to tell the disciples the news. Second, the women instantly fall at Jesus' feet and worship him. In neither case is there any pause or hesitation. This stands in contrast to the decidedly mixed reaction of the eleven male disciples gathered on the mountain in verse 17.

Question 7. N. T. Wright states the question this way: "Did they hesitate over, or doubt, whether it was truly Jesus? Or did they hesitate over, or doubt, whether they, as good Jewish monotheists, believing in YHWH as the one true God, should actually *worship* Jesus?" (*Matthew for Everyone: Chapters 16-28* [Louisville, KY: Westminster John Knox, 2004], p. 206). If they wondered whether it was really Jesus, we might conclude that they did not believe the women's message and had failed to put their report together with Jesus' promises to meet them in Galilee after he rose from the dead (Mt 26:32). If they wondered what they should do when they saw the risen Lord, then perhaps their hesitation is more understandable. After all, worship was reserved for the one God. On the other hand, the fact that some of them *did* worship the risen Lord when they saw him is remarkable in light of Judaism's deep commitment to monotheism. Perhaps both of these factors were at work. Those who believed it was really Jesus sensed that worship was the only proper response; those who weren't sure were afraid to bow down.

Question 10. The charge to make disciples is not restricted to ordained ministers! We all can do our part in spreading the good news about who Jesus is and what he has done for us. Help participants identify the particular gifts and abilities they bring to this mission.

Question 12. Be sure to highlight that if we trust that Christ is faithful to his promises, we will find strength to give ourselves fully to his mission, knowing (1) that we do so in his power and under his authority, not our own, and (2) that he is with us every step of the way.

Study 6. Bold Allegiance. Acts 2:22-36.

Purpose: To encourage bold allegiance and witness to the risen Lord.

Question 1. Will Willimon says, "A good speech can turn us inside out" (*Acts*, Interpretation [Louisville, KY: Westminster John Knox, 1988], p. 34). That seems to be the intention (and perhaps the effect) of Peter's sermon on Pentecost. He doesn't sugarcoat his message. He openly implicates his audience in the death of the Messiah. It's likely many hearers would have been shocked by Peter's boldness and offended by much of what he had to say. Encourage participants to share honestly how Peter's message might have sounded to them.

Question 2. The straightforward answer is that Peter accuses the Israelites of crucifying Jesus of Nazareth despite the fact that they witnessed his great wonders. Verse 23 complicates matters. Though Peter finds his fellow Israelites guilty of murder, he also acknowledges that they simply acted out what had been determined long ago by their God. Rather than digressing into a long conversation about divine sovereignty and human free will, it's more helpful simply to point out why Peter made this claim at all. He wants to insist that God's redemptive purposes cannot be thwarted by human sin. God planned all along to use the inevitable sin of his people to bring about their salvation. Yes, they are guilty. But because of God's great wisdom and mercy, there is hope for them through the very man they crucified. It's a beautiful irony.

Question 3. This is admittedly a difficult question, but one worth pondering. Participants may be inclined to jump to answers like, "Because he was God!" While this truth ought to be affirmed without hesitation, the text allows us to explore Peter's claim more closely. Peter explains himself by citing Psalm 16 and arguing that Jesus could not be held in the grave because God had promised long ago through the lips of David himself that the "holy one"—the great Messiah—would not "see decay."

Question 4. Peter preaches from Psalms 16 and 110. David was upheld by the Jewish people as the ideal king of Israel. His psalms were both well known and sacred among the people. If Peter could argue that David spoke specifically of this Jesus of Nazareth and explain significant truths about Jesus' resurrection (Ps 16) and exaltation (Ps 110) through the familiar words of the psalms, then he just might gain a hearing.

Question 5. The central point is quite simple: Jesus is the true King of Israel. David's songs find their ultimate fulfillment in Jesus. He is the one they've been waiting for!

Question 6. Help participants to think about this concept in our world. We most often use the term in legal settings. You might ask if anyone has ever served as a witness in court. What did that entail? The important points to cover are that witnesses (1) see, hear or otherwise experience something in person, and (2) are called on to testify to what they have seen, heard or experienced before others who were not there for the event. In other words, the *passive*, sometimes accidental, occurrence of witnessing an event leads to an *active*, intentional, testimony about the event. Sometimes this active testimony is dangerous—as in cases where someone witnesses a murder. Speaking up may put a person in danger. Much of this applies to the biblical concept of "witness" as well.

Question 9. People often struggle to understand the presence and influence of the Holy Spirit in their lives. As you reflect on this passage, you may ask if there have been times when the Spirit has helped them to speak the good news or show the love of Christ to someone. Often the Spirit shows up in more subtle ways than on Pentecost, but that doesn't mean he isn't just as much at work now as back then.

Question 10. These terms are important for understanding Peter's radical message. *Messiah* means "anointed one." Among the first-century Jewish people, this title was reserved for the promised king who was to come and restore the kingdom to Israel, freeing the people from their oppressors (see Acts 1:6). The fact that Jesus had died but was then raised and exalted to a place of power with God demonstrated his true kingship, even though at this point it was not what the people expected. The term *Lord* is much broader and probably indicated that Christ's rule extends beyond Israel to the rest of the world. He sits at the right hand of God not only as "Israel's true and final king" but as "the world's rightful sovereign" as well (N. T. Wright, *Acts for Everyone* [Louisville, KY: Westminster John Knox, 2008], p. 38).

Questions 11-12. Simply put, if Jesus is the true Ruler of all, then to him alone we owe our allegiance. Encourage participants to be specific about the meaning of Jesus' lordship in their lives: what it means to honor him, obey him, be devoted to him and trust his sovereign care of the world. Then try to draw out the implications for boldly letting others in on this great truth, just as Peter did on the day of Pentecost.

Study 7. A Meaningful Life. 1 Corinthians 15:35-58.

Purpose: To discover the enduring value of present life and work in the promise of the resurrection.

Question 1. This is an important question to begin the conversation about this text. Many lifelong believers have ideas about the afterlife that are completely foreign to the Scriptures. Try to get a sense for whether bodily resurrection is an important feature of future existence to your participants. Invite them to allow this text to challenge how they understand life after death.

Questions 2-3. (1) Paul uses the analogies of seeds (vv. 36-38) to emphasize the way God will transform a seed in the ground into a new body appropriate to (continuous with) its kind. (2) He talks about human flesh versus different kinds of animal flesh (v. 39) to emphasize that "not all flesh is the same." (3) And he speaks of heavenly bodies (stars, planets) versus earthly bodies (vv. 40-41) to emphasize that some kinds of bodies have more "splendor" than others. He will go on to make all of these points about the relationship between our current "natural" bodies and our future "spiritual" bodies.

Question 4. The earthly body is "perishable" and characterized by "weakness" and "dishonor." The spiritual body is "imperishable" and characterized by "power" and "glory." It's important to understand that by "spiritual" body, Paul does not mean immaterial or ghostly body—as though there will be no physical substance. All of Paul's analogies point to a material body, but one much more wonderful than our current body that is prone to death and decay.

Question 5. The point is to direct our attention to Christ as the one who has gone before us in this great bodily transformation and has therefore set the pattern for what we will become. Just as we took after the "first Adam" in being subject to corruption and death, so we will take after the "last Adam" in experiencing resurrection and life.

Question 7. The quotation is taken from a beautiful picture of God's intended future for his people in Isaiah 25:8. In some ways Paul's "mystery" is just an elaboration of how God intends to bring about the glorious future he has promised. Death will be "swallowed up" when our perishable bodies are changed and we become like the risen Christ in power, glory and immortality.

Question 9. We might expect Paul to say something like, "Therefore, brothers and sisters, look forward to the day of your transformation, for the Lord will fulfill his promise." But he doesn't say this. This is a surprising turn—

and yet it's not. Remember the seed analogy from verse 37? There is continuity between the first body and the second, even though God effects a wonderful transformation.

Questions 10-12. These questions are designed as an extended reflection on verse 58, since it offers such a rich insight on the significance of the resurrection for our present Christian lives. N. T. Wright is eloquent here:

> If it is true that God is going to transform this present world, and renew our whole selves, bodies included, then what we do in the present time with our bodies, and with our world, matters. . . . How God will take our prayer, our art, our love, our writing, our political action, our music, our honesty, our daily work, our pastoral care, our teaching, our whole selves—how God will take this and weave its varied strands into the glorious tapestry of his new creation, we can at present have no idea. (N. T. Wright, *Paul for Everyone: 1 Corinthians* [Louisville, KY: Westminster John Knox, 2004], p. 228)

Study 8. Freedom to Live. Romans 8:1-11.

Purpose: To discover that the Spirit of the risen Lord frees people to live for God.

Question 1. Hopefully the initial group discussion or personal reflection set up this question nicely by raising some contrasting perspectives on the nature of freedom. Encourage participants to articulate both what we are free "from" (e.g., sin) and what we are free "for" (e.g., love of God). If your group needs some extra guidance, you might raise some common related Scripture verses, such as John 8:32 or Galatians 5:1.

Question 3. Free from our well-deserved guilty sentence (see Rom 7), we no longer feel compelled to obey God out of fear of punishment or retribution. Since the law no longer has power to condemn us, neither can sin deceive and snare us the way it used to. Instead, we live our lives for God out of gratitude for the forgiveness and love he has shown us in Christ. Obedience now flows out of thankfulness and joy in the Spirit. The is the way the "law" of the Spirit works—exactly the opposite of the "law of sin and death"!

Question 4. One commentator draws this distinction nicely: "It is helpful to remember in this discussion that Paul uses the words 'flesh' and 'spirit' not to designate two parts of human nature but rather to represent two ways of living. . . . Life in the flesh is essentially life carried on under the lordship of the sinful self. It is a life of self-idolatry. Life in the Spirit, on the other hand, is life set free from bondage to self and sin" (Paul Achtemeier, *Romans*, Interpretation [Louisville, KY: Westminster John Knox, 1986], pp. 131-32). In other words, we should not make the mistake of thinking that things "the Spirit desires" are

invisible or immaterial (belonging to the human soul or spirit), nor that the things "the flesh desires" have to do with the physical, material body. Rather, the things of the Spirit are related to true and abundant life both now and forever, while the things of the flesh are related to physical and spiritual death. **Question 7.** Participants may be feeling this tension already, which is important to acknowledge. This passage might seem to speak of an ideal existence, where those indwelt by the Spirit always live by the Spirit. But that is so often not our experience. Explore with your group why this might be the case. What's wonderful about the Spirit-led life is that even when we don't get it right, there is still *no condemnation* for us. (This truth should be emphasized!) We rest in Christ's perfect obedience, not our own. Sometimes we forget this and are swept up into sin's old games of guilt and deceit. Here's how the law of the Spirit works: *even when we fail* we are spurred on to further gratitude to God for his forgiveness, and are thus walking by the Spirit once again. The cycle of sin and fear is broken. We are truly free.
Question 9. Our bodies are "dead" because sin has robbed them of life. But because of Christ, this death isn't the end of the story. Grant Osborne explains: "This is not death *to* sin (as in 6:2, 11), but death *because of* sin, so it must refer to the fact that as sinners we still must face the death of the (physical) *body* (cf. 5:12). . . . The body faces death, but that will lead to resurrection" (*Romans*, IVP New Testament Commentary [Downers Grove, IL: InterVarsity Press, 2004], p. 201).

Study 9. New Clothes. Colossians 3:1-17.
Purpose: To learn to lay aside the old garments and put on the new clothes of the risen Lord.
Question 2. This is a big question, but it is central to understanding this passage. One author explains it this way: "Paul thus sketches the believers' life in Christ with three bold strokes encompassing past, present, and future. Believers have died and have been raised with Christ; in the present their life is hidden with Christ; and at his coming they will be revealed in glory with him" (Marianne Meye Thompson, *Colossians and Philemon*, Two Horizons New Testament Commentary [Grand Rapids: Eerdmans, 2005], p. 69). She goes on to identify the key theological idea here as "participation" in Christ. It's not that we imitate Jesus but that we are somehow actually united with him in his reality. We are identified with him in a very real way, and thus Christ's identity is our identity. This is who we are as Christians at the most fundamental level.
Question 3. The "things above" are precisely the realities proclaimed here— our union with Christ and participation in his risen life. We are not to be

distracted by unimportant things that will not last—"earthly things" that pull our attention away from our identity in Christ.

Question 6. The earthly things must go because they are not suitable for life as the people of the risen and exalted Christ. We are called to a higher place, where sinful, self-centered habits and vices no longer define us.

Question 8. Verse 11 is truly astounding. If we thought our identity in Christ was a personal matter, Paul makes sure we catch the bigger vision. Since we all share in the one risen Lord's past, present and future, all the social distinctions that seem so important in this world (class, ethnicity, etc.) are completely done away with in Christ. These distinctions have no bearing on our true identity, for "Christ *is* all, and is *in* all." You may want to discuss with participants how well they feel their church community does in living out this reality.

Question 10. One common struggle with lists of Christian virtues (as in vv. 12-14) is that we begin to feel overwhelmed and inadequate. That's asking an awful lot. Who could possibly display all these wonderful qualities? The answer, of course, is Jesus Christ. And since we live in Christ—indeed, since our lives are "hidden" with him (v. 3)—we will show forth these qualities too.

Question 11. We are instructed to draw on the riches of Christ's forgiveness (v. 13), Christ's peace (v. 15), and Christ's Word (v. 16) as we clothe ourselves. Because we live in and with the risen Christ (vv. 1-4), we wear what he's wearing—almost like sharing the wardrobe of the risen King.

Question 12. You may first need to discuss what it means to act in the "name" of Christ.

Study 10: All Things New. Revelation 21:1-8.

Purpose: To form a hope for the day when death is expelled and the whole earth is made new.

Question 1. You may want to ask participants to close their eyes as you read through the passage again. Ask what images are most vivid to them and what reactions accompany each image. Are they comforted? Troubled? Confused?

Questions 2-3. The straightforward answer is that they pass away. But take some time to explore what this means. You might refer to 2 Corinthians 5:17 as a possible parallel passage. The notion that "the old" or "the first" things pass away does not necessarily mean that there is no trace of anything we've ever known. It may simply mean that those things characteristic of the old broken order (see v. 4) vanish so that everything may find life and purpose again in God's renewed world. The first heaven and earth must pass away because they are broken. They must disappear to make way for God's glorious future.

Question 4. Perhaps the best way to answer this question is to look ahead to Revelation 21:22-23 and 22:3-5. Although God's presence is among us now through his Spirit, God and the Lamb are still veiled from our sight. In the new creation described here, it seems that God's presence will be more immediate, even visible to our renewed and transformed eyes. Perhaps we will experience him tangibly—see by his light, be warmed by his presence and bow down at his throne.

Question 6. So that we don't wander too far off the subject of resurrection, it is important to remember the slain Lamb who sits on the throne in the book of Revelation. The one who went through death and came out the other side as the exalted Lord is the only one with the authority to banish death from God's world. Because of Christ's victory over death, its days are numbered.

Question 7. This may seem like a trick question, but it's definitely not. "All things" is rather vague. You may want to ask more specific questions: Are animals made new? Plants and oceans? What about houses and cities? Try to help participants understand the grand scope of God's new creation. If your group struggles with this, it may be worth reflecting briefly on Romans 8:19-22.

Question 10. The idea of "overcoming" or "conquering" is important in Revelation. It shows up in each of the seven letters to the Asian churches in chapters 1–3 and seems to refer to those remaining faithful to Christ in the face of great difficulty or persecution. While most of us do not face the same kind of threats from kings and emperors that first-century Christians did, we are still called to remain faithful to Christ in the face of tremendous challenges to our faith. The promise of the waters of life and the inheritance of the new creation is offered as a gift to all who cling to Christ rather than turning away when hard times come.

Question 11. Chances are that verse 8 will make some participants squirm— or at least raise an eyebrow or two. But this is actually central to the glorious, death-free, life-abounding existence of God's new creation. Those who would tear at the fabric of this new world—those who are set against God and his good purposes—will have *no place* there. They must "pass away" with the old order because they are so invested in its warped ways that they cannot extricate themselves from it. So there is another place appointed for them. Since we know so little about this place, it is probably not fruitful to speculate about its nature. The chief point here is not the lake of fire but that God will steadfastly protect his new creation against anything that poses a threat to its everlasting beauty and joy.

Kristie Berglund holds an MDiv from Fuller Seminary and an MA in theological studies from Regent College. Formerly an employee of InterVarsity Press, she currently resides in Southern California, where she is preparing for pastoral ministry in the Presbyterian Church (USA).